50 Pudding Recipes for Home

By: Kelly Johnson

Table of Contents

- Classic Vanilla Pudding
- Chocolate Pudding
- Banana Pudding
- Rice Pudding
- Tapioca Pudding
- Butterscotch Pudding
- Bread Pudding
- Chia Seed Pudding
- Coconut Pudding
- Mango Pudding
- Pumpkin Pudding
- Sticky Toffee Pudding
- Caramel Pudding
- Lemon Pudding
- Peanut Butter Pudding
- Mocha Pudding
- Matcha Green Tea Pudding
- Almond Milk Pudding
- Maple Pudding
- Eggnog Pudding
- Avocado Chocolate Pudding
- Raspberry Pudding
- Dulce de Leche Pudding
- Honey Pudding
- Black Sesame Pudding
- Strawberry Pudding
- Blueberry Pudding
- Cinnamon Pudding
- Apple Cinnamon Bread Pudding
- Espresso Pudding
- Hazelnut Pudding
- Orange Cream Pudding
- Pineapple Pudding
- Gingerbread Pudding
- Sweet Potato Pudding

- Cherry Almond Pudding
- Bourbon Bread Pudding
- Yogurt Pudding
- Cashew Pudding
- Sago Pudding
- Pistachio Pudding
- Oatmeal Pudding
- Chocolate Chip Pudding
- Cheesecake Pudding
- Vanilla Bean Pudding
- Cranberry Pudding
- Dark Chocolate Raspberry Pudding
- Carrot Pudding
- Pecan Pie Pudding
- Marshmallow Pudding

Classic Vanilla Pudding

Ingredients:

- 2 cups whole milk
- ½ cup sugar
- 3 tbsp cornstarch
- ¼ tsp salt
- 2 egg yolks
- 2 tbsp butter
- 2 tsp vanilla extract

Instructions:

1. In a saucepan, whisk sugar, cornstarch, and salt.
2. Slowly whisk in milk and cook over medium heat, stirring constantly, until thickened.
3. Temper egg yolks by whisking in a little hot milk mixture, then add back to the pan.
4. Cook for 2 more minutes, remove from heat, and stir in butter and vanilla.
5. Chill before serving.

Chocolate Pudding

Ingredients:

- 2 cups milk
- ½ cup sugar
- ¼ cup cocoa powder
- 3 tbsp cornstarch
- ¼ tsp salt
- 1 tsp vanilla extract
- 2 oz dark chocolate, chopped

Instructions:

1. In a saucepan, whisk sugar, cocoa powder, cornstarch, and salt.
2. Slowly whisk in milk and heat until thickened.
3. Remove from heat and stir in vanilla and chopped chocolate.
4. Chill before serving.

Banana Pudding

Ingredients:

- 3 ripe bananas, sliced
- 2 cups whole milk
- ½ cup sugar
- 3 tbsp cornstarch
- ¼ tsp salt
- 2 egg yolks
- 2 tbsp butter
- 1 tsp vanilla extract
- Vanilla wafers

Instructions:

1. Cook the vanilla pudding base (same as Vanilla Pudding recipe).
2. Let cool slightly, then layer with banana slices and vanilla wafers.
3. Chill for 2 hours before serving.

Rice Pudding

Ingredients:

- ½ cup rice
- 2 cups milk
- ¼ cup sugar
- 1 tsp vanilla extract
- ¼ tsp cinnamon
- ¼ cup raisins (optional)

Instructions:

1. Cook rice in milk over low heat until tender.
2. Stir in sugar, vanilla, and cinnamon.
3. Add raisins if desired and simmer for 5 minutes.
4. Serve warm or chilled.

Tapioca Pudding

Ingredients:

- ½ cup small tapioca pearls
- 2 cups milk
- ¼ cup sugar
- 1 egg yolk
- 1 tsp vanilla extract

Instructions:

1. Soak tapioca pearls in water for 30 minutes, then drain.
2. Heat milk and sugar over medium heat, then stir in tapioca.
3. Simmer for 15 minutes, stirring.
4. Whisk a little hot mixture into the egg yolk, then stir back into the pudding.
5. Cook for 5 more minutes, then add vanilla.

Butterscotch Pudding

Ingredients:

- 2 cups milk
- ½ cup brown sugar
- 3 tbsp cornstarch
- ¼ tsp salt
- 2 tbsp butter
- 1 tsp vanilla extract

Instructions:

1. In a saucepan, whisk brown sugar, cornstarch, and salt.
2. Slowly whisk in milk and cook until thickened.
3. Remove from heat and stir in butter and vanilla.
4. Chill before serving.

Bread Pudding

Ingredients:

- 4 cups cubed bread
- 2 cups milk
- ½ cup sugar
- 2 eggs
- 1 tsp cinnamon
- ½ tsp vanilla extract
- ¼ cup raisins (optional)

Instructions:

1. Preheat oven to 350°F (175°C). Grease a baking dish.
2. Whisk milk, sugar, eggs, cinnamon, and vanilla.
3. Add bread cubes and soak for 15 minutes. Stir in raisins if using.
4. Bake for 40 minutes until golden.

Chia Seed Pudding

Ingredients:

- 1 cup milk (or almond milk)
- 3 tbsp chia seeds
- 1 tbsp honey
- ½ tsp vanilla extract

Instructions:

1. Mix all ingredients in a jar and refrigerate overnight.
2. Stir and serve chilled.

Coconut Pudding

Ingredients:

- 2 cups coconut milk
- ½ cup sugar
- 3 tbsp cornstarch
- ¼ tsp salt
- 1 tsp vanilla extract
- ¼ cup shredded coconut

Instructions:

1. Heat coconut milk, sugar, cornstarch, and salt over medium heat, whisking until thickened.
2. Remove from heat, stir in vanilla and shredded coconut.
3. Chill before serving.

Mango Pudding

Ingredients:

- 2 ripe mangoes, blended
- 1 cup coconut milk
- ¼ cup sugar
- 1 tbsp gelatin (dissolved in 2 tbsp hot water)

Instructions:

1. Mix mango puree, coconut milk, and sugar.
2. Stir in dissolved gelatin and mix well.
3. Pour into molds and chill for 4 hours.

Pumpkin Pudding

Ingredients:

- 1 cup pumpkin puree
- 2 cups milk
- ½ cup sugar
- 3 tbsp cornstarch
- 1 tsp cinnamon
- ½ tsp nutmeg
- ½ tsp vanilla extract

Instructions:

1. Heat milk, sugar, cornstarch, cinnamon, and nutmeg over medium heat until thickened.
2. Stir in pumpkin puree and vanilla.
3. Chill before serving.

Sticky Toffee Pudding

Ingredients:

Cake:

- 1 cup chopped dates
- 1 tsp baking soda
- 1 cup boiling water
- ½ cup butter, softened
- ¾ cup brown sugar
- 2 eggs
- 1 ½ cups flour
- 1 tsp baking powder
- ½ tsp cinnamon

Toffee Sauce:

- ½ cup butter
- 1 cup brown sugar
- ¾ cup heavy cream
- 1 tsp vanilla extract

Instructions:

1. Preheat oven to 350°F (175°C). Grease a baking dish.
2. Soak dates in boiling water with baking soda for 10 minutes.
3. Cream butter and sugar, add eggs, then mix in flour, baking powder, cinnamon, and date mixture.
4. Pour into dish and bake for 30 minutes.
5. For sauce, heat butter, sugar, and cream until thickened. Stir in vanilla.
6. Pour warm toffee sauce over pudding before serving.

Caramel Pudding

Ingredients:

- 2 cups milk
- ½ cup sugar
- 3 tbsp cornstarch
- ¼ tsp salt
- ¼ cup caramel sauce
- 1 tsp vanilla extract

Instructions:

1. Whisk sugar, cornstarch, and salt in a saucepan. Slowly add milk and cook over medium heat until thickened.
2. Remove from heat and stir in caramel sauce and vanilla.
3. Chill before serving.

Lemon Pudding

Ingredients:

- 2 cups milk
- ½ cup sugar
- 3 tbsp cornstarch
- Zest of 1 lemon
- 2 tbsp lemon juice
- 1 tsp vanilla extract

Instructions:

1. In a saucepan, mix sugar, cornstarch, and lemon zest.
2. Slowly whisk in milk and cook until thickened.
3. Remove from heat and stir in lemon juice and vanilla.
4. Chill before serving.

Peanut Butter Pudding

Ingredients:

- 2 cups milk
- ½ cup peanut butter
- ½ cup sugar
- 3 tbsp cornstarch
- ¼ tsp salt
- 1 tsp vanilla extract

Instructions:

1. Whisk sugar, cornstarch, and salt in a saucepan. Slowly whisk in milk and cook over medium heat.
2. Stir in peanut butter and cook until thickened.
3. Remove from heat and add vanilla.
4. Chill before serving.

Mocha Pudding

Ingredients:

- 2 cups milk
- ¼ cup sugar
- 2 tbsp cocoa powder
- 2 tbsp cornstarch
- 1 tbsp instant coffee
- 1 tsp vanilla extract

Instructions:

1. In a saucepan, whisk sugar, cocoa, cornstarch, and instant coffee.
2. Slowly whisk in milk and cook over medium heat until thickened.
3. Remove from heat, stir in vanilla, and chill before serving.

Matcha Green Tea Pudding

Ingredients:

- 2 cups milk
- ¼ cup sugar
- 2 tbsp cornstarch
- 1 tbsp matcha powder
- 1 tsp vanilla extract

Instructions:

1. Whisk sugar, cornstarch, and matcha powder in a saucepan.
2. Slowly add milk and cook over medium heat until thickened.
3. Remove from heat, stir in vanilla, and chill before serving.

Almond Milk Pudding

Ingredients:

- 2 cups almond milk
- ¼ cup sugar
- 3 tbsp cornstarch
- ¼ tsp salt
- 1 tsp vanilla extract

Instructions:

1. Mix sugar, cornstarch, and salt in a saucepan. Slowly add almond milk.
2. Cook over medium heat until thickened.
3. Remove from heat, stir in vanilla, and chill before serving.

Maple Pudding

Ingredients:

- 2 cups milk
- ½ cup maple syrup
- 3 tbsp cornstarch
- ¼ tsp salt
- 1 tsp vanilla extract

Instructions:

1. In a saucepan, whisk cornstarch, salt, and milk. Cook over medium heat until thickened.
2. Stir in maple syrup and vanilla.
3. Chill before serving.

Eggnog Pudding

Ingredients:

- 2 cups eggnog
- ¼ cup sugar
- 3 tbsp cornstarch
- ½ tsp nutmeg
- 1 tsp vanilla extract

Instructions:

1. In a saucepan, whisk sugar, cornstarch, and nutmeg.
2. Slowly add eggnog and cook over medium heat until thickened.
3. Remove from heat, stir in vanilla, and chill before serving.

Avocado Chocolate Pudding

Ingredients:

- 2 ripe avocados
- ¼ cup cocoa powder
- ¼ cup honey or maple syrup
- ½ cup milk or almond milk
- 1 tsp vanilla extract

Instructions:

1. Blend all ingredients until smooth.
2. Chill for at least 1 hour before serving.

Raspberry Pudding

Ingredients:

- 2 cups milk
- ½ cup sugar
- 3 tbsp cornstarch
- 1 cup fresh or frozen raspberries
- 1 tsp vanilla extract

Instructions:

1. Blend raspberries into a puree and strain to remove seeds.
2. In a saucepan, whisk sugar and cornstarch, then slowly add milk.
3. Cook over medium heat until thickened.
4. Stir in raspberry puree and vanilla, then chill before serving.

Dulce de Leche Pudding

Ingredients:

- 2 cups milk
- ½ cup dulce de leche
- 3 tbsp cornstarch
- ¼ tsp salt
- 1 tsp vanilla extract

Instructions:

1. In a saucepan, whisk cornstarch and salt. Slowly add milk and cook until thickened.
2. Stir in dulce de leche and cook for 2 more minutes.
3. Remove from heat, add vanilla, and chill before serving.

Honey Pudding

Ingredients:

- 2 cups milk
- ¼ cup honey
- 3 tbsp cornstarch
- ¼ tsp salt
- 1 tsp vanilla extract

Instructions:

1. In a saucepan, whisk cornstarch and salt. Slowly add milk and cook until thickened.
2. Stir in honey and vanilla, then chill before serving.

Black Sesame Pudding

Ingredients:

- 2 cups milk
- ¼ cup sugar
- 3 tbsp cornstarch
- 2 tbsp black sesame paste
- 1 tsp vanilla extract

Instructions:

1. In a saucepan, whisk sugar and cornstarch. Slowly add milk and cook until thickened.
2. Stir in black sesame paste and vanilla, then chill before serving.

Strawberry Pudding

Ingredients:

- 2 cups milk
- ½ cup sugar
- 3 tbsp cornstarch
- 1 cup fresh or frozen strawberries, blended
- 1 tsp vanilla extract

Instructions:

1. Blend strawberries into a puree.
2. In a saucepan, whisk sugar and cornstarch, then slowly add milk.
3. Cook over medium heat until thickened.
4. Stir in strawberry puree and vanilla, then chill before serving.

Blueberry Pudding

Ingredients:

- 2 cups milk
- ½ cup sugar
- 3 tbsp cornstarch
- 1 cup blueberries, blended
- 1 tsp vanilla extract

Instructions:

1. Blend blueberries into a puree.
2. In a saucepan, whisk sugar and cornstarch, then slowly add milk.
3. Cook over medium heat until thickened.
4. Stir in blueberry puree and vanilla, then chill before serving.

Cinnamon Pudding

Ingredients:

- 2 cups milk
- ½ cup sugar
- 3 tbsp cornstarch
- 1 tsp cinnamon
- 1 tsp vanilla extract

Instructions:

1. In a saucepan, whisk sugar, cornstarch, and cinnamon. Slowly add milk and cook until thickened.
2. Stir in vanilla and chill before serving.

Apple Cinnamon Bread Pudding

Ingredients:

- 4 cups cubed bread
- 2 cups milk
- ½ cup sugar
- 1 apple, diced
- 2 eggs
- 1 tsp cinnamon
- 1 tsp vanilla extract

Instructions:

1. Preheat oven to 350°F (175°C). Grease a baking dish.
2. Whisk milk, sugar, eggs, cinnamon, and vanilla.
3. Stir in bread and apples, then let soak for 15 minutes.
4. Bake for 40 minutes until golden.

Espresso Pudding

Ingredients:

- 2 cups milk
- ½ cup sugar
- 3 tbsp cornstarch
- 1 tbsp instant espresso powder
- 1 tsp vanilla extract

Instructions:

1. In a saucepan, whisk sugar, cornstarch, and espresso powder. Slowly add milk and cook until thickened.
2. Stir in vanilla and chill before serving.

Hazelnut Pudding

Ingredients:

- 2 cups milk
- ½ cup sugar
- 3 tbsp cornstarch
- ¼ cup hazelnut butter
- 1 tsp vanilla extract

Instructions:

1. In a saucepan, whisk sugar and cornstarch. Slowly add milk and cook until thickened.
2. Stir in hazelnut butter and vanilla, then chill before serving.

Orange Cream Pudding

Ingredients:

- 2 cups milk
- ½ cup sugar
- 3 tbsp cornstarch
- Zest of 1 orange
- 2 tbsp orange juice
- 1 tsp vanilla extract

Instructions:

1. In a saucepan, whisk sugar, cornstarch, and orange zest. Slowly add milk and cook until thickened.
2. Stir in orange juice and vanilla, then chill before serving.

Pineapple Pudding

Ingredients:

- 2 cups milk
- ½ cup sugar
- 3 tbsp cornstarch
- 1 cup pineapple puree
- 1 tsp vanilla extract

Instructions:

1. Blend pineapple into a puree.
2. In a saucepan, whisk sugar and cornstarch, then slowly add milk.
3. Cook over medium heat until thickened.
4. Stir in pineapple puree and vanilla, then chill before serving.

Gingerbread Pudding

Ingredients:

- 2 cups milk
- ½ cup brown sugar
- 3 tbsp cornstarch
- 1 tsp cinnamon
- 1 tsp ginger
- ¼ tsp nutmeg
- 1 tsp vanilla extract

Instructions:

1. In a saucepan, whisk sugar, cornstarch, cinnamon, ginger, and nutmeg.
2. Slowly whisk in milk and cook over medium heat until thickened.
3. Remove from heat, stir in vanilla, and chill before serving.

Sweet Potato Pudding

Ingredients:

- 2 cups mashed sweet potatoes
- 1 cup milk
- ½ cup sugar
- 2 eggs
- 1 tsp cinnamon
- ½ tsp nutmeg
- 1 tsp vanilla extract

Instructions:

1. Preheat oven to 350°F (175°C). Grease a baking dish.
2. Mix all ingredients until smooth.
3. Pour into dish and bake for 40 minutes.

Cherry Almond Pudding

Ingredients:

- 2 cups milk
- ½ cup sugar
- 3 tbsp cornstarch
- ½ cup chopped cherries
- ¼ tsp almond extract
- 1 tsp vanilla extract

Instructions:

1. In a saucepan, whisk sugar and cornstarch. Slowly add milk and cook over medium heat until thickened.
2. Stir in cherries, almond extract, and vanilla.
3. Chill before serving.

Bourbon Bread Pudding

Ingredients:

- 4 cups cubed bread
- 2 cups milk
- ½ cup sugar
- 2 eggs
- 2 tbsp bourbon
- 1 tsp cinnamon
- 1 tsp vanilla extract

Instructions:

1. Preheat oven to 350°F (175°C). Grease a baking dish.
2. Whisk milk, sugar, eggs, bourbon, cinnamon, and vanilla.
3. Stir in bread and let soak for 15 minutes.
4. Bake for 40 minutes until golden.

Yogurt Pudding

Ingredients:

- 2 cups plain yogurt
- ¼ cup honey
- 3 tbsp cornstarch
- ½ tsp vanilla extract

Instructions:

1. In a saucepan, whisk honey and cornstarch. Slowly add yogurt and cook over medium heat until thickened.
2. Stir in vanilla and chill before serving.

Cashew Pudding

Ingredients:

- 2 cups cashew milk
- ½ cup sugar
- 3 tbsp cornstarch
- ¼ cup cashew butter
- 1 tsp vanilla extract

Instructions:

1. In a saucepan, whisk sugar and cornstarch. Slowly add cashew milk and cook until thickened.
2. Stir in cashew butter and vanilla.
3. Chill before serving.

Sago Pudding

Ingredients:

- ½ cup sago pearls
- 2 cups coconut milk
- ½ cup sugar
- 1 tsp vanilla extract

Instructions:

1. Soak sago pearls in water for 30 minutes.
2. Drain and cook in coconut milk over medium heat until translucent.
3. Stir in sugar and vanilla, then chill before serving.

Pistachio Pudding

Ingredients:

- 2 cups milk
- ½ cup sugar
- 3 tbsp cornstarch
- ¼ cup ground pistachios
- 1 tsp vanilla extract

Instructions:

1. In a saucepan, whisk sugar and cornstarch. Slowly add milk and cook over medium heat until thickened.
2. Stir in pistachios and vanilla.
3. Chill before serving.

Oatmeal Pudding

Ingredients:

- 2 cups milk
- ½ cup rolled oats
- ¼ cup sugar
- ½ tsp cinnamon
- 1 tsp vanilla extract

Instructions:

1. In a saucepan, cook oats, milk, sugar, and cinnamon over medium heat until thick.
2. Stir in vanilla and chill before serving.

Chocolate Chip Pudding

Ingredients:

- 2 cups milk
- ½ cup sugar
- 3 tbsp cornstarch
- ½ cup chocolate chips
- 1 tsp vanilla extract

Instructions:

1. In a saucepan, whisk sugar and cornstarch. Slowly add milk and cook over medium heat until thickened.
2. Stir in chocolate chips and vanilla.
3. Chill before serving.

Cheesecake Pudding

Ingredients:

- 2 cups milk
- ½ cup cream cheese, softened
- ½ cup sugar
- 3 tbsp cornstarch
- 1 tsp vanilla extract

Instructions:

1. In a saucepan, whisk sugar and cornstarch. Slowly add milk and cook over medium heat until thickened.
2. Stir in cream cheese and vanilla until smooth.
3. Chill before serving.

Vanilla Bean Pudding

Ingredients:

- 2 cups milk
- ½ cup sugar
- 3 tbsp cornstarch
- 1 vanilla bean (or 1 tsp vanilla extract)

Instructions:

1. Split the vanilla bean and scrape out seeds.
2. In a saucepan, whisk sugar and cornstarch. Slowly add milk and cook over medium heat until thickened.
3. Stir in vanilla bean seeds (or extract) and chill before serving.

Cranberry Pudding

Ingredients:

- 2 cups milk
- ½ cup sugar
- 3 tbsp cornstarch
- ½ cup cranberry puree
- 1 tsp vanilla extract

Instructions:

1. Blend cranberries into a puree.
2. In a saucepan, whisk sugar and cornstarch. Slowly add milk and cook over medium heat until thickened.
3. Stir in cranberry puree and vanilla, then chill before serving.

Dark Chocolate Raspberry Pudding

Ingredients:

- 2 cups milk
- ½ cup sugar
- 3 tbsp cornstarch
- ½ cup dark chocolate, melted
- ¼ cup raspberry puree
- 1 tsp vanilla extract

Instructions:

1. Blend raspberries into a puree.
2. In a saucepan, whisk sugar and cornstarch. Slowly add milk and cook over medium heat until thickened.
3. Stir in melted dark chocolate, raspberry puree, and vanilla.
4. Chill before serving.

Carrot Pudding

Ingredients:

- 2 cups milk
- ½ cup sugar
- 3 tbsp cornstarch
- ½ cup finely grated carrots
- ½ tsp cinnamon
- 1 tsp vanilla extract

Instructions:

1. In a saucepan, whisk sugar, cornstarch, and cinnamon. Slowly add milk and cook over medium heat until thickened.
2. Stir in grated carrots and vanilla, then chill before serving.

Pecan Pie Pudding

Ingredients:

- 2 cups milk
- ½ cup brown sugar
- 3 tbsp cornstarch
- ¼ tsp salt
- ½ cup chopped pecans
- 1 tsp vanilla extract

Instructions:

1. In a saucepan, whisk brown sugar, cornstarch, and salt. Slowly add milk and cook over medium heat until thickened.
2. Stir in chopped pecans and vanilla, then chill before serving.

Marshmallow Pudding

Ingredients:

- 2 cups milk
- ½ cup sugar
- 3 tbsp cornstarch
- 1 cup mini marshmallows
- 1 tsp vanilla extract

Instructions:

1. In a saucepan, whisk sugar and cornstarch. Slowly add milk and cook over medium heat until thickened.
2. Stir in marshmallows until melted, then add vanilla.
3. Chill before serving.